Paige Tate

Beauty in the Bible
ADULT COLORING BOOK

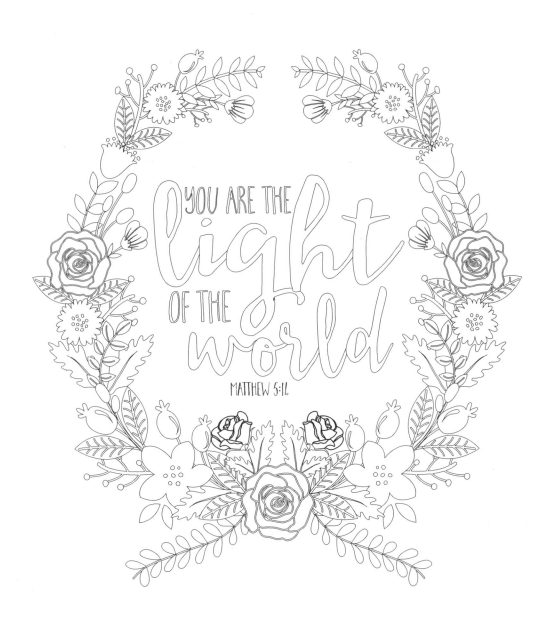

YOU ARE THE light OF THE world

MATTHEW 5:14

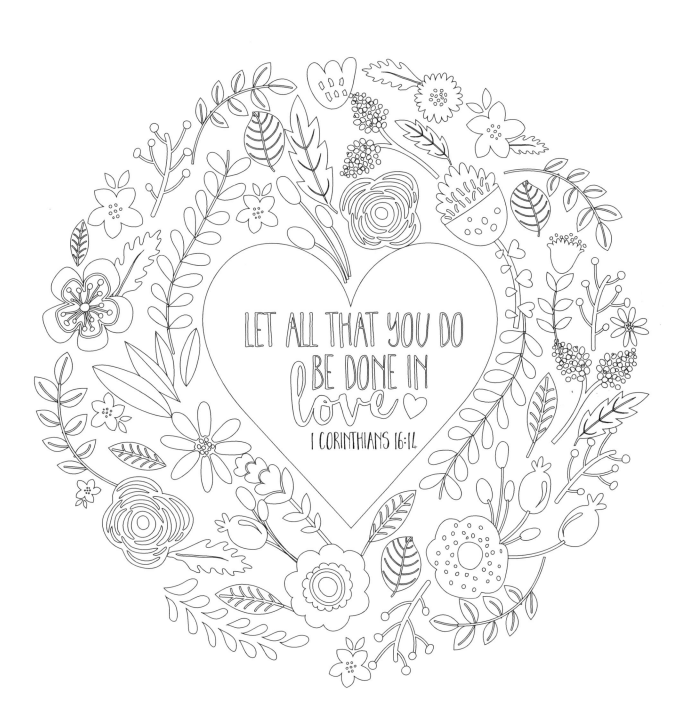

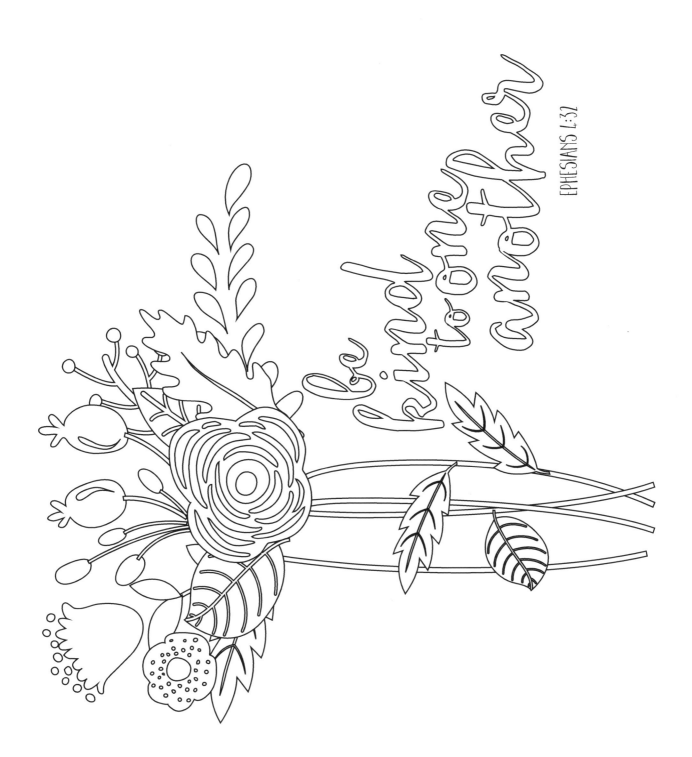

Be kind to one another

EPHESIANS 4:32

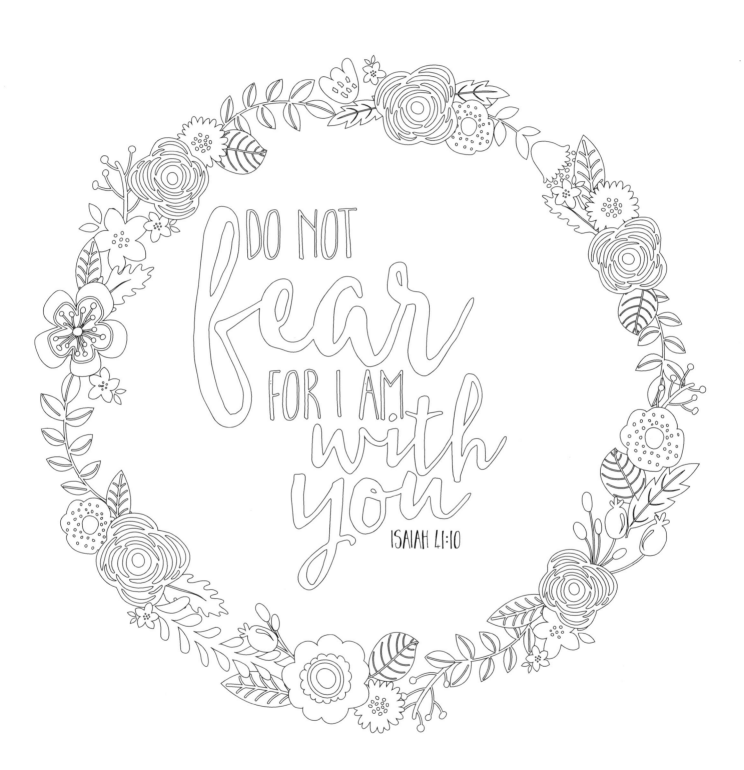

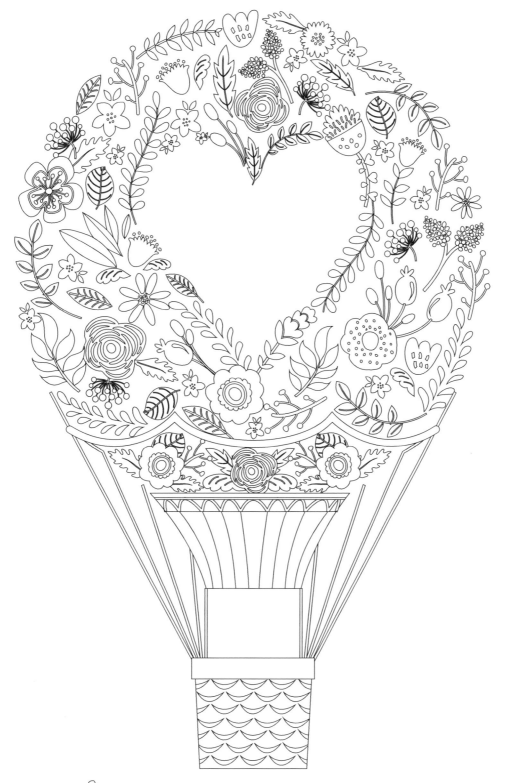

BE strong AND courageous
FOR THE Lord WILL BE WITH YOU WHEREVER
YOU go   JOSHUA 1:9

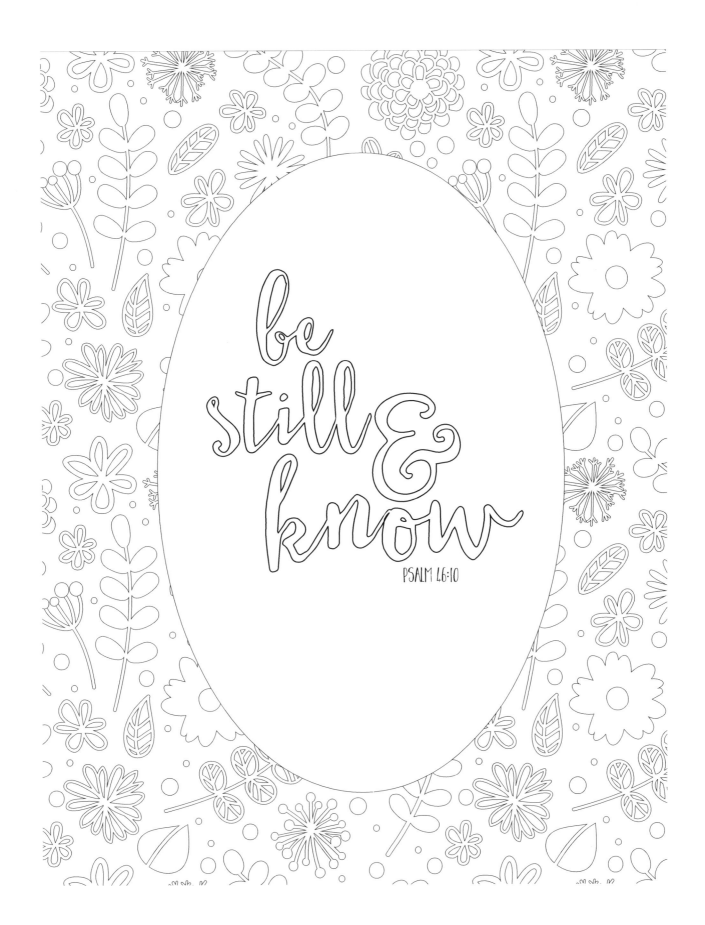

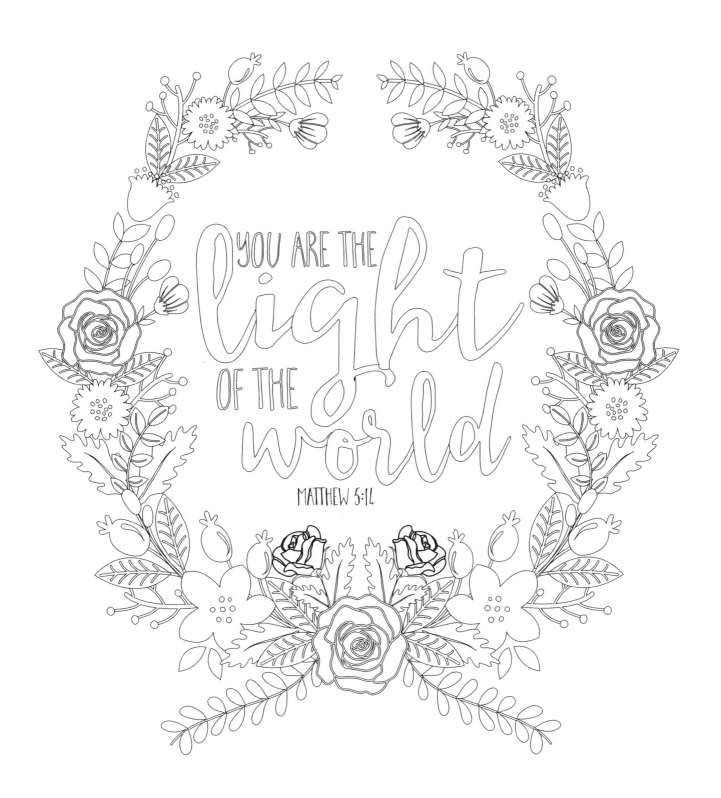

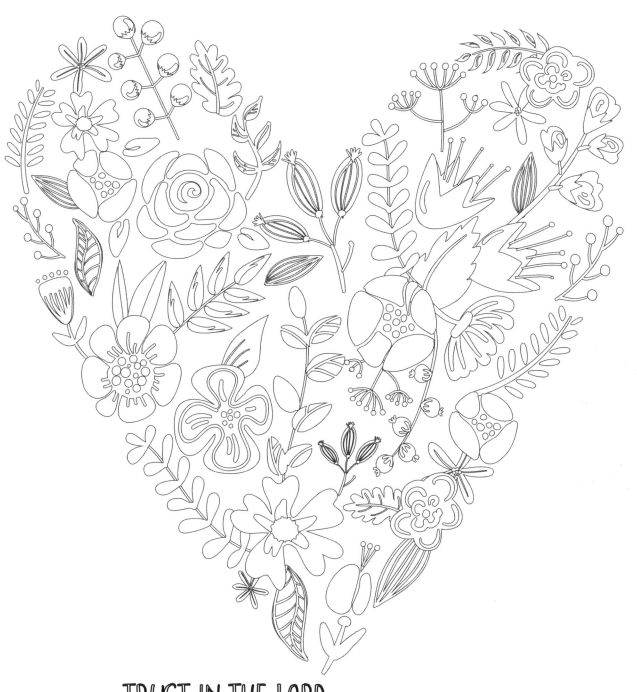

TRUST IN THE LORD
WITH ALL YOUR
heart
PROVERBS 3:5

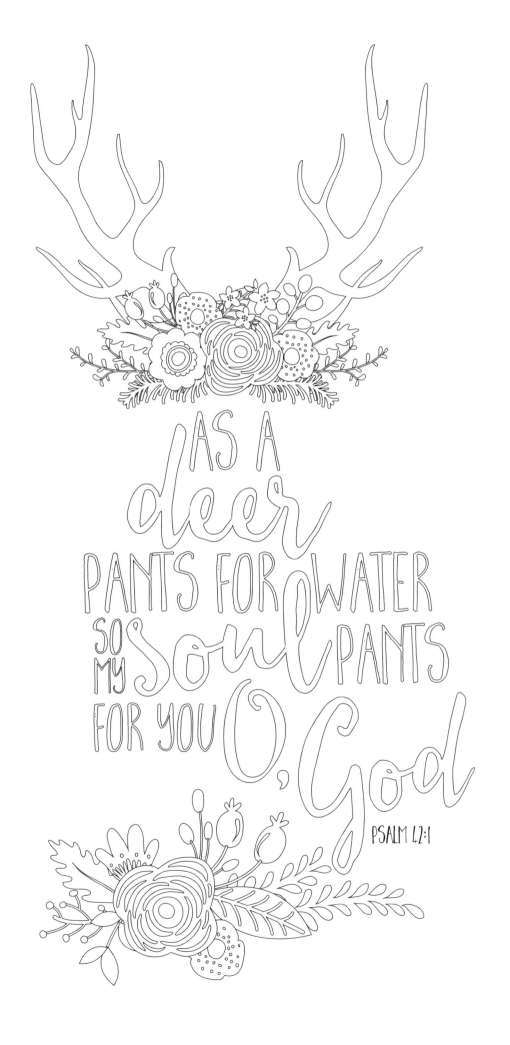

AS A *deer* PANTS FOR WATER SO MY *soul* PANTS FOR YOU O, *God*

PSALM 42:1

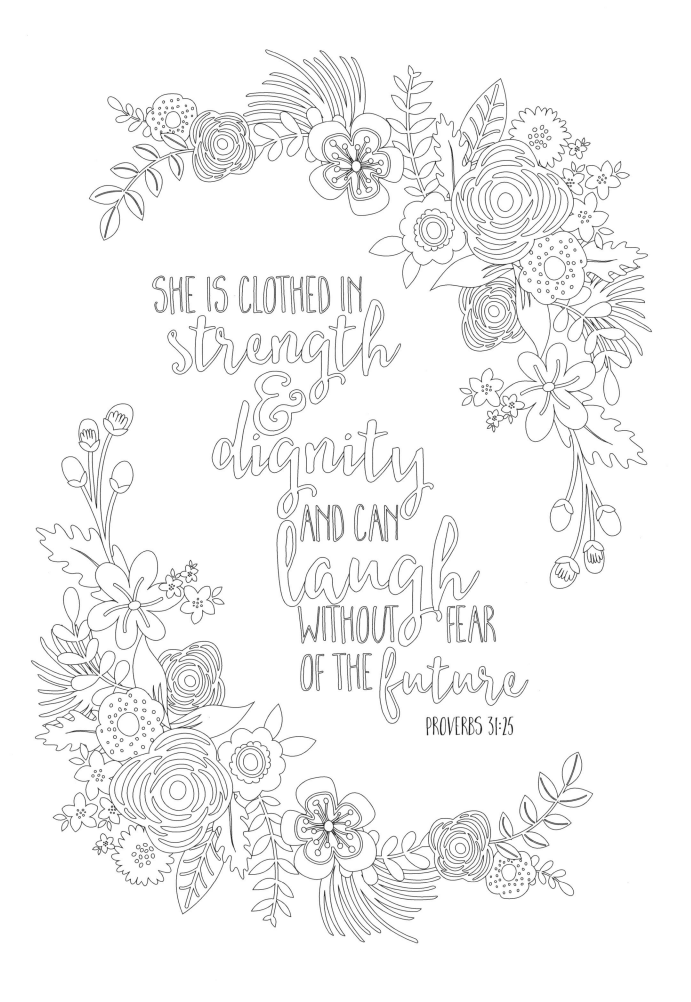

SHE IS CLOTHED IN *strength* & *dignity* AND CAN *laugh* WITHOUT FEAR OF THE *future*

PROVERBS 31:25

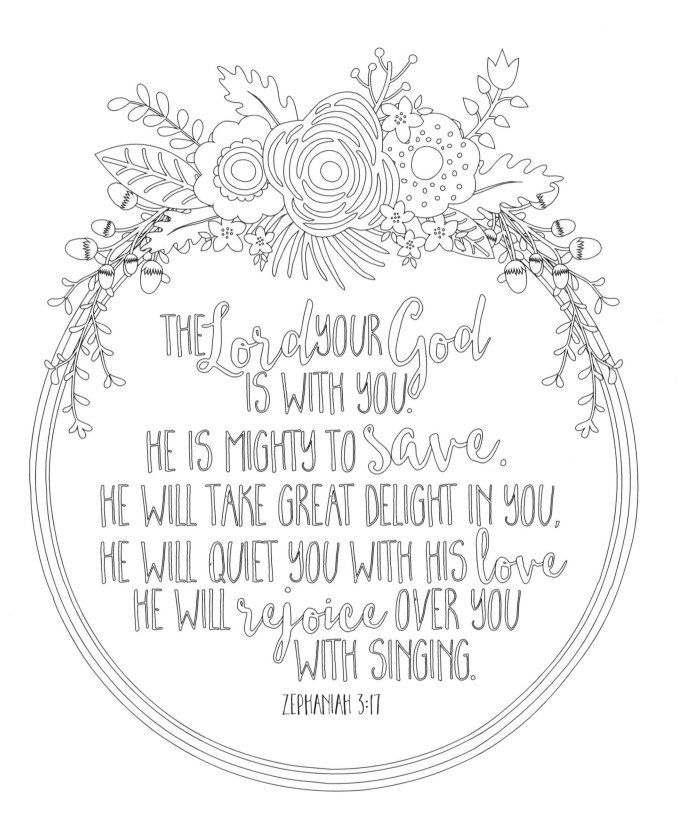

THE Lord YOUR God
IS WITH YOU.
HE IS MIGHTY TO Save.
HE WILL TAKE GREAT DELIGHT IN YOU,
HE WILL QUIET YOU WITH HIS love
HE WILL rejoice OVER YOU
WITH SINGING.

ZEPHANIAH 3:17

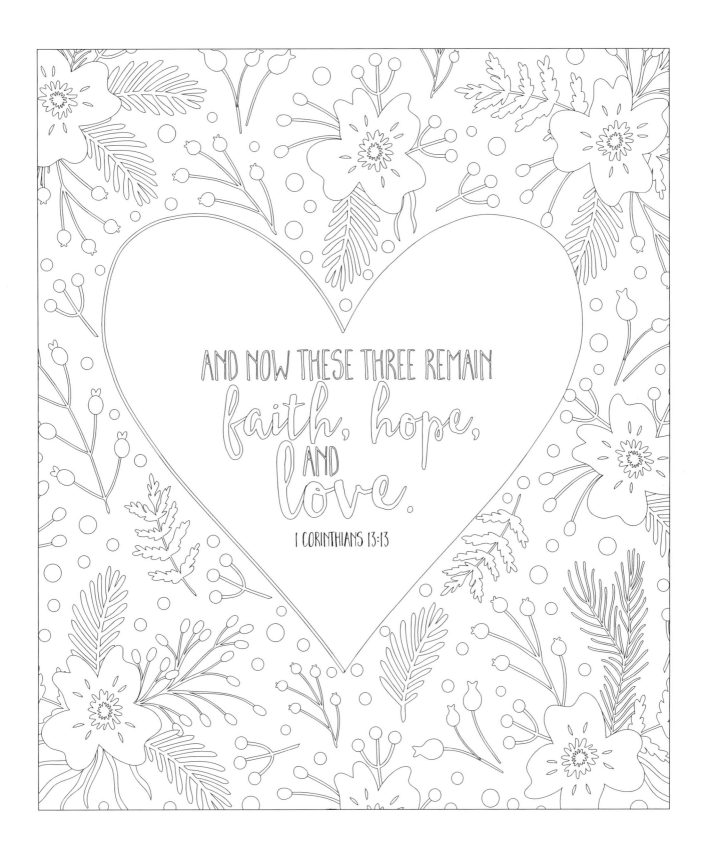

AND NOW THESE THREE REMAIN
faith, hope,
AND
love.

1 CORINTHIANS 13:13

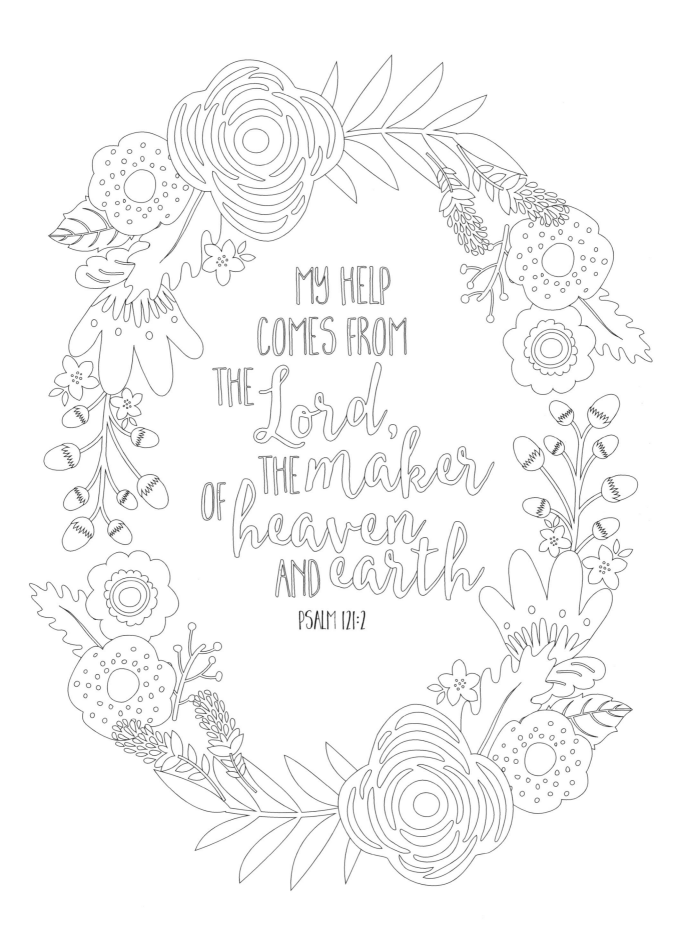

MY HELP COMES FROM THE Lord, THE maker OF heaven AND earth

PSALM 121:2

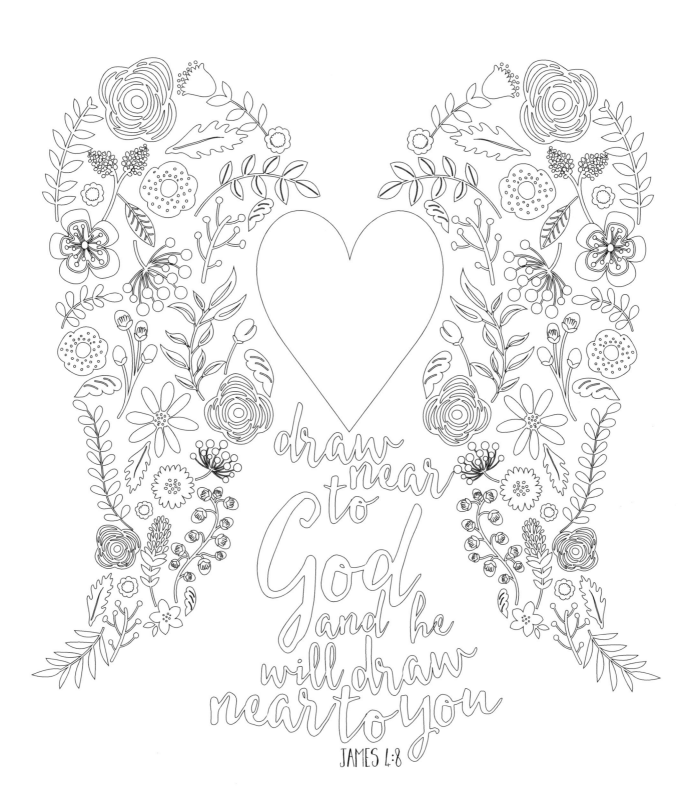

draw near to God and he will draw near to you

JAMES 4:8

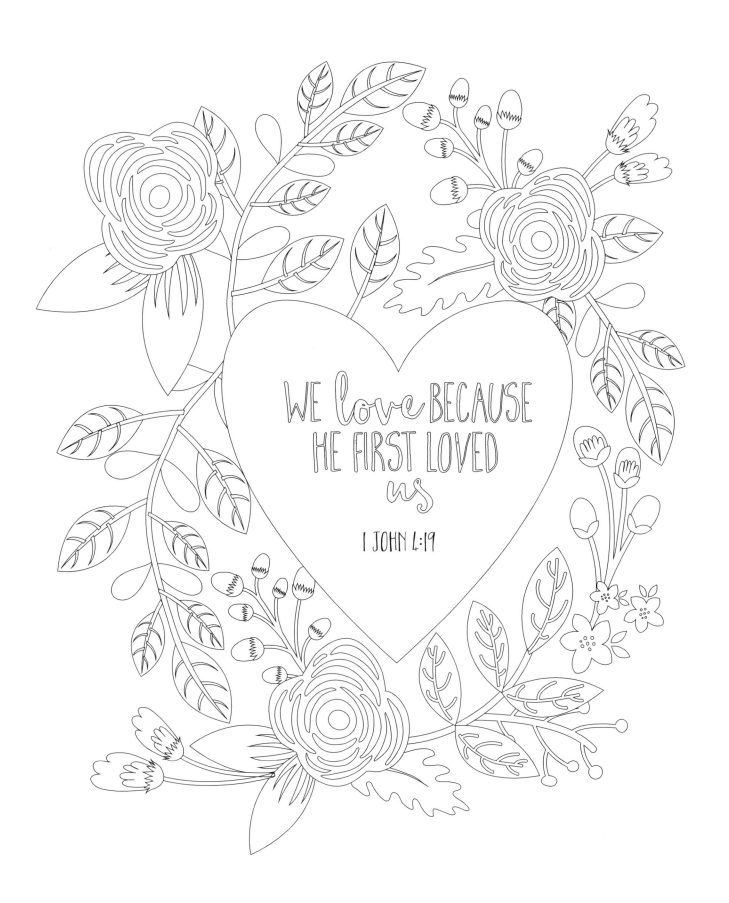

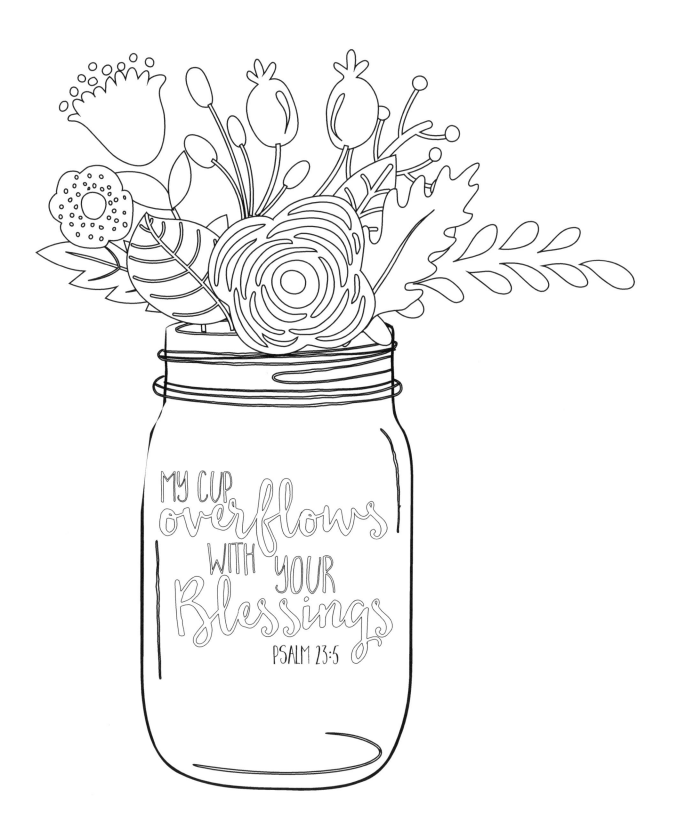

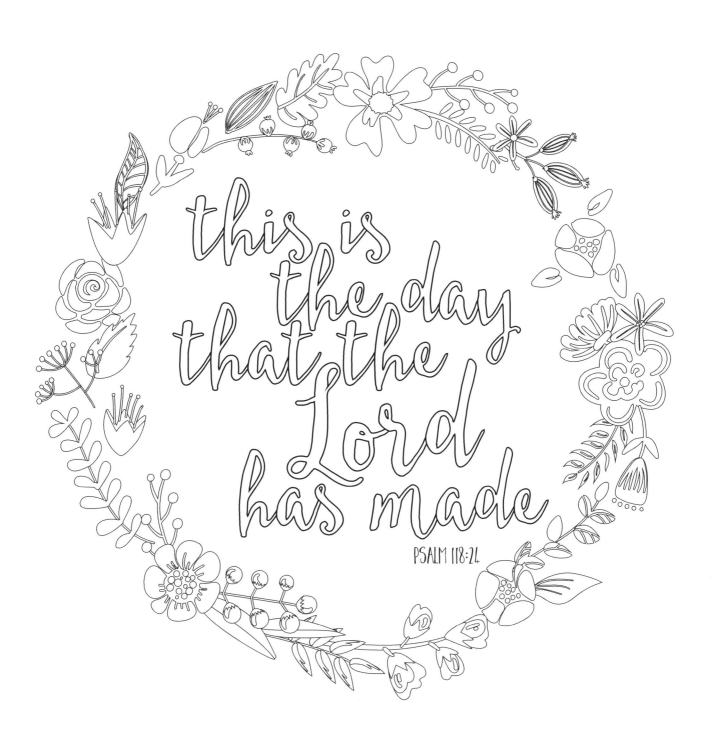

this is
the day
that the
Lord
has made

PSALM 118:24

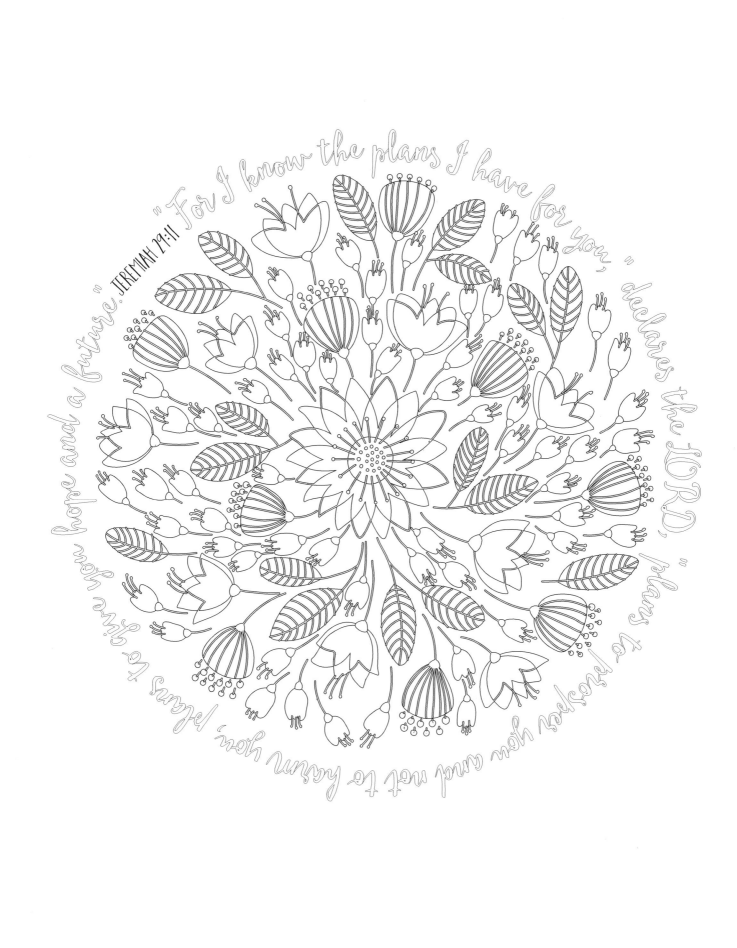

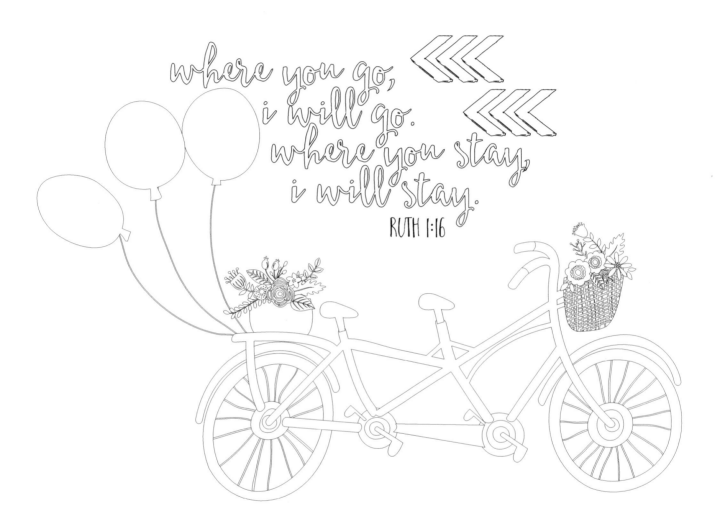

where you go,
i will go.
where you stay,
i will stay.
RUTH 1:16

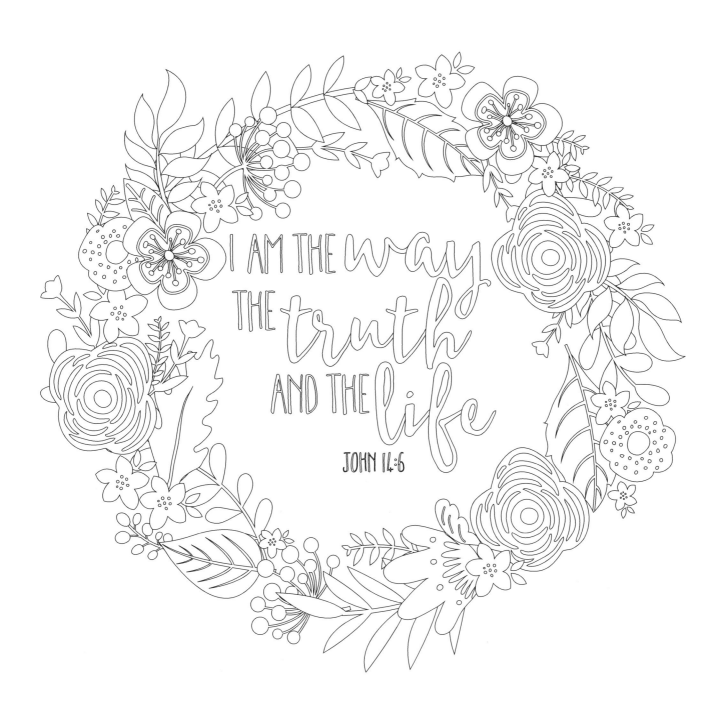

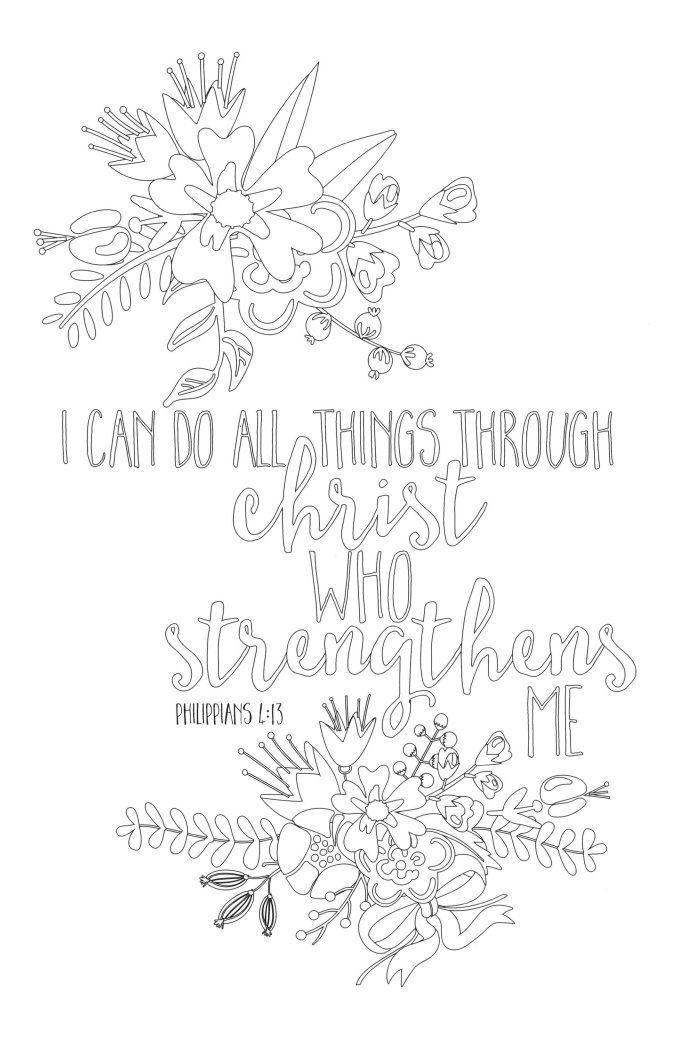

I CAN DO ALL THINGS THROUGH *christ* WHO *strengthens* ME

PHILIPPIANS 4:13

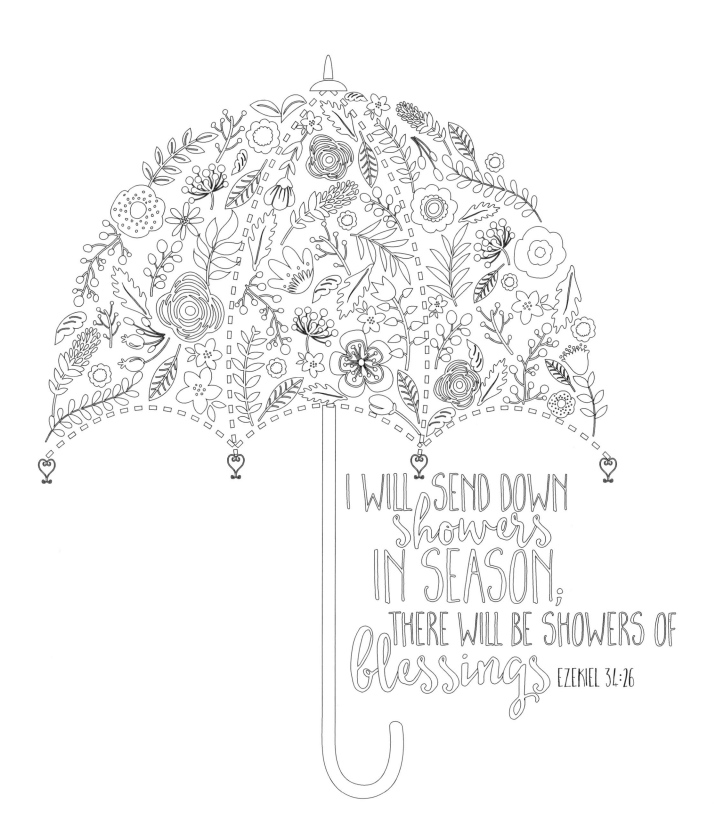

I WILL SEND DOWN *showers* IN SEASON; THERE WILL BE SHOWERS OF *blessings* EZEKIEL 34:26

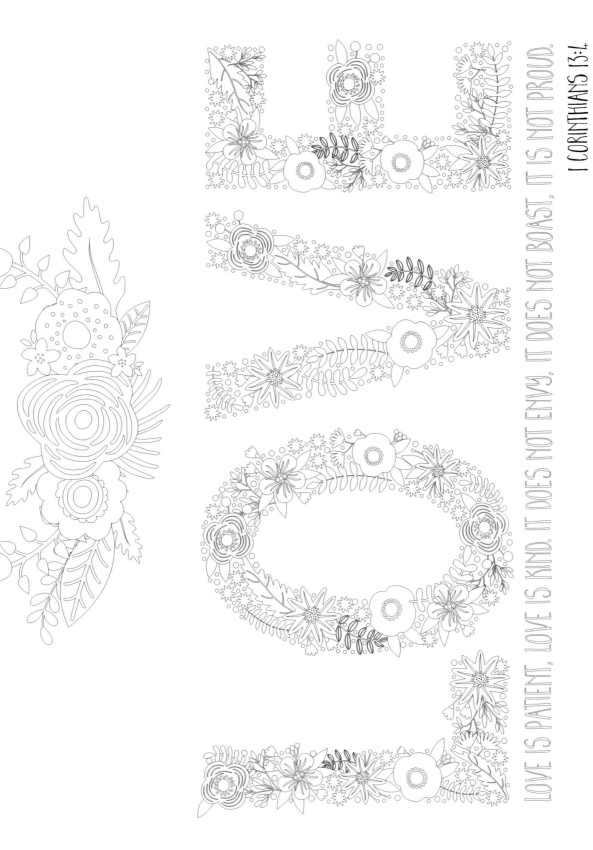

LOVE IS PATIENT, LOVE IS KIND. IT DOES NOT ENVY, IT DOES NOT BOAST, IT IS NOT PROUD.

I CORINTHIANS 13:4

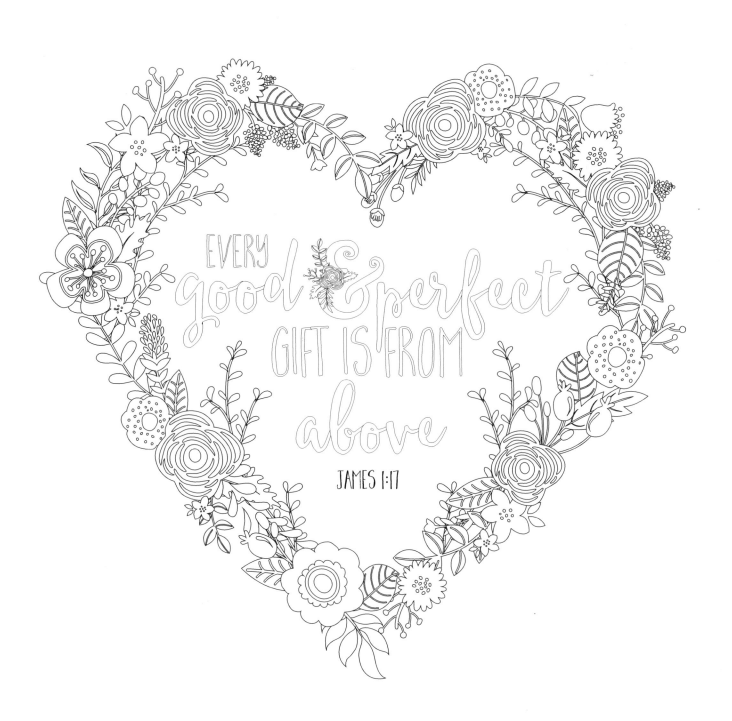

EVERY *good* & *perfect* GIFT IS FROM *above*

JAMES 1:17

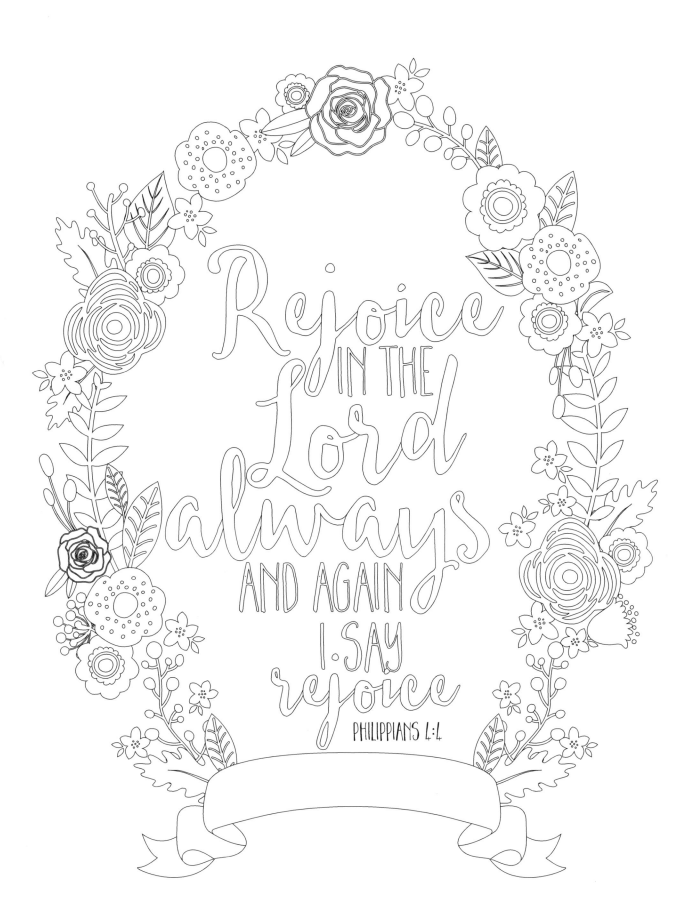

Made in the USA
Middletown, DE
03 July 2020